FRUIT CAKE

POEMS

LISA BADNER

FRUITCAKE
Copyright © 2022 Lisa Badner
All Rights Reserved.
Published by Unsolicited Press.
Printed in the United States of America.
First Edition.

No part of this book may be used or reproduced in any manner whatsoever without written permission except in the case of brief quotations embodied in critical articles or reviews.

Attention schools and businesses: for discounted copies on large orders, please contact the publisher directly.

For information contact:
Unsolicited Press
Portland, Oregon
www.unsolicitedpress.com
orders@unsolicitedpress.com
619-354-8005

Cover Designer: Kathryn Gerhardt
Editors: S.R. Stewart and Robin Ann Lee
ISBN: 978-1-956692-23-5

For Arnold and Barbara

Table of Contents

I

ON THE G TRAIN	8
FACEBOOK FRIENDS	9
ERIC, MY DEAD FRIEND	10
FUCK PASSOVER	12
SUBWAY JUDGE	13
MUSIC FESTIVAL	15
FRUITCAKE	18
UNEMPLOYMENT JUDGE	19
CHRISTMAS AT THE KOSHER BAKERY	20
THIS IS NOT AN OBITUARY	22
TAXI COURT	25

II

PHONE CALL FROM EX-THERAPIST	28
ALL BABIES CRY	31
MOM'S BIRTHDAY AT THE WOODSTOCK HOUSE	32
MR BEAGELMAN:	33
RAINY SUNDAY WITH TODDLER	34

BITCHES' BRITCHES	36
PARENTS' BED AT THE WOODSTOCK HOUSE	38
MOMMY WRITING POEM NOW	39
AGE RELATED	41

III

NORO VIRUS	44
YOUR FATHER HAS ALZHEIMER'S	46
I HAD A WINDOW	47
BEDTIME POET	49
CAREER CHANGE	50
ON MY FORTY-FIFTH BIRTHDAY	52
SHRIMPS	53
SUBWAY SEAT	55
A SUNDAY WALK IN AUTUMN	56
WATCHING ADOPTION VIDEO WITH MY EIGHT YEAR OLD	57

IV

SPAM	60
MACAROONS – THE LAST DAYS	61
PARENT/TEACHER CONFERENCE	63
EXTRACTION	65

SHIVA CALL	67
NOBODY PUT A GUN TO MY HEAD	68
FIFTY	70

I

ON THE G TRAIN

A woman scratches her inner ear
with a ballpoint pen.
The man next to me is sleeping.
People date for months
before sleeping and grooming together,
yet this guy is bobbing onto my shoulder.
Yesterday, a woman clipped her nails.
I see a man with terrible growths
on his face and neck.
Wearing a wedding band.
All people have genitals,
I am nauseous.
A woman with ripped socks and flip-flops
opens her tote bag,
resting on the filthy floor.
She could throw up
or have a bomb.
She takes out a book on world peace.
I am not comforted.

FACEBOOK FRIENDS

Fran is my friend on Facebook.
In the '90s, Fran and I were roommates, then girlfriends.
Dina is my friend on Facebook too.
I cheated on Fran to be with Dina.
It was in Jerusalem and very dramatic.
Fran can see that I am friends with Dina on Facebook
because Dina is on my list of friends.
I friend Fran's new girlfriend Ellie,
since we are all pretty friendly.
Ellie friends Dina. Ellie doesn't know Dina,
but Ellie friends all of her Facebook friends' friends.
Ellie is friends with Alan.
Alan and Ellie were boyfriend and girlfriend in the '80s,
before Ellie was gay.
Alan friends me. I have never met Alan,
but I was girlfriends with his first wife, Deb,
when Deb was still dabbling.
We weren't very friendly after that.
Alan and Deb are friends on Facebook,
though I hear Deb may have recently died.
Fran and Ellie and Dina are also friends with Deb on Facebook.
Tomorrow I'm going to friend Deb too.

ERIC, MY DEAD FRIEND

When I was twenty,
I cried to my older friend Eric

that my life was a failure.
He, at twenty-four, assured me

it would all work out.
We smoked cigarettes,

drank Pepsi all night,
and (awkwardly) made out.

Eric, a feminist,
joined Men Stopping Rape

cried when he watched the news.
Tried to be gay

(said it was less misogynist)
and we went to lesbian music concerts.

After he finished his PhD,
he turned weird, distant,

workaholic, never wanted to chat.
Didn't seem so feminist anymore,

wrote lots of articles I couldn't understand
(they were quantitative.)

He kept smoking (I quit.)
Eric was famous —

in an academic kind of way.
I decided not to call him anymore.

And he never called me.
I wanted to tell him, *fuck you,*

for not calling.

FUCK PASSOVER

Fuck Passover, my mother says,

everyone else gets the good holidays.
Jenny gets Thanksgiving,
Libby gets Rosh Hashanah,
and I get stuck with Passover.
Fuck Passover. Daddy can have his Seder
in the bathroom.

SUBWAY JUDGE

Two peed,
but called it passing water.
One spat, one smoked,
fourteen couldn't swipe.
Nine doubled up,
four crawled under, six jumped over.
Seven walked between cars: two were faint,
three smelled a bum,
one had diabetes and one had gout.
Two wheelchairs, two walkers, six strollers,
four high wheels, six gates. One chased by a rapist.
One fake snake.
Four cried. Three for real.
One sleeper, two leaners, three feet, six bags.
Eight tourists. Two suits.
Eleven on welfare. One Croatian.
One Jew. I was caught snacking three times,
under my desk. I was
twice admonished through glass,
to use "system," "tender," "fare media,"
to wear my badge.
My phone vibrated once.

I was told four times,
turn it off.

MUSIC FESTIVAL

Shortly after dropping out of graduate school,
and after my mother sent my father
from New York to rescue me
from the Midwest lesbians,

I attended a festival.
There were eight thousand women.
Most were lesbian.
Many were naked.

I went topless
but not bottomless.
I went with friends,
who quickly found new friends.

I sat by myself.
Too stiff to dance to the music.
Even though it was a music festival.
I watched others dance and make out:

Tall skinny blonds, wearing nothing
but hiking shoes and belts, swaying

to Holly Near with large shaved Amazons
wearing rope sandals and cloth fig leaves.

I waited in long lines. Alone.
Lines to use the "porta janes" — which reeked,
lines for showers, which were cold,
Lines for food, which hosted bacteria — making several sick.

And then the thunder —
Sweet Honey in the Rock
rained out. Lost —
searching for my tent,

I wandered through
the *S* and *M* encampment:
women in spiked dog collars
huddling under tarps.

When I got to my tent,
the floor was covered
with filthy rainwater,
and floating cigarette butts.

My tentmate —
my only hope of intimacy
had moved out
to a dry tent.

FRUITCAKE

My father makes macaroons for a living.
They are a popular product and quite healthy.
The macaroons are named for my sister, Jenny.
"Jennies" they are called. "Jennies Macaroons."
My father made a "Lisa Fruitcake" once.
Shrink wrapped. In a drab beige box with gray lettering.
Small pieces of shriveled raisins, candied dates. Nuts,
some too hard to chew. It was dry. Fell apart like "sawdust"
one customer wrote, "embarrassed me in front of my
        guests."
The Lisa Fruitcake never made it into a trade show, or an ad.
Rejected unanimously by the distributors,
the Lisa Fruitcake was a resounding failure.

UNEMPLOYMENT JUDGE

A pharmacist screwed up
my transaction.
Couldn't figure out
the co-pay for my Zoloft.
I made a scene.
That was a few months ago.
Today, the same guy
sits in my courtroom,
begging for his unemployment benefits
because he was fired.
Not from what happened with me,
but some other stupidity.
I am the judge.
The judge on Zoloft.
The judge on Zoloft who decides
whether the pharmacist
gets benefits.

CHRISTMAS AT THE KOSHER BAKERY

The workers laugh about the time
my father's ding-dong
hung out of his shorts,

his upper body engulfed in the macaroon mixer.
My mother eats a whole flan.
I open my gifts. Empty faux crystal

perfume bottles, Santa paperweights.
Workers go back to the canning machines,
drunk on Coquito, and I pack up samples
to send to health gurus and kosher gyms.

The boxes are chewed up.
Rats discovered the new bars. Ate through
sheetrock to get to them. *Never corner a rat*,
my father says, *it will go for your throat.*

Madeline, the bookkeeper's daughter
is foreman. She weighs 200 pounds
and has tattoos. Ramona runs the can machine.
She had a baby last year using Madeline's egg.

I get a call from the adoption agency.
They say a child is ready for me.
I don't have a crib or a diaper.
Just a yellow fever shot.

I tell my mother but not my father.
Well there goes your whole life, she says.

My father drives me home.
Crams his Saab with bakery trash.
We drive through Williamsburg looking for a place
       to dump it.
It's raining. The Satmar Hasidim wear garbage bags
around their big furry hats.

White knee socks
and furry hats. One watches
my father add to a heap on Lee Avenue.
Dad says not to worry, it's shabbos and he can't write.

When I'm home, my neighbor
Avi rings the bell. He's off his meds.
Life is a terminal illness,
he tells me, *but it's a nice evening,*
so let's take a walk.

THIS IS NOT AN OBITUARY

For Claudia Card

Claudia, you asked me in advance to write your obituary.
You gave me your thirty-seven-page single-spaced CV.
Now that the time has come,
I have not written an obituary.

After the biopsy results last year,
you said I would inherit your music library.
I used to play piano.
I stopped playing piano in 1984.

You nominated me for a graduate fellowship.
You said I would have been a good philosopher.
I got the fellowship. Thank you.
Then I dropped out.

I went back to New York, and eventually to law school
to pursue a mediocre career. After your lung surgery
you told your other visitors that I was a *judge*.
You seemed so proud. Claudia, I kept telling you,
administrative judge.

In the '90s I took you on a walking tour
all over Manhattan.
You developed plantar fasciitis
from the hard city pavement.

I took your ethics class in 1984. You still held the chalk like
    the cigarettes
you used to chain-smoke. Your mother died of lung cancer.
You told me how your family was so poor she barely went to
    the doctor—
the lung tumor protruded from her chest by the time she
    got someone
to look at it. So in 1989
I lied when you asked me if I smoked.

The last time I ever saw you,
I hugged you goodbye when my taxi arrived
to take me to the airport.
You were in bed, cancer in your brain, maybe your spine.
My heavy backpack fell over me
onto your abdomen.

When they moved you to hospice
you said on the phone you'd rather I come see you again

at this new facility
then come to your funeral.

I didn't see you at hospice.
I didn't go to your funeral.

TAXI COURT

They call me judge.
Talk about hacks and specs,
seizures and blues.
It all eludes me.
A limo driver says it's a conspiracy.
Medallions and cops — takes off his shoe —
In my country, this means I tell the truth,
licks the bottom.
They read Taxi News and look at their watches.
My decisions pile up
while I try passwords on the computer.
downandout123, neerdowell456.
Finally, ihatelaw789, gets me in.

I find everybody guilty.

II

PHONE CALL FROM EX-THERAPIST

She was my object relation for thirteen years.
My rapprochement.
My transference.
My borderline bouncing board.

Until I could no longer afford
even the rent control equivalent
to therapy.
So when a text message appears on my phone
from my ex-therapist saying *we have to talk*,
I get a lump in my throat.

Does she have cancer?
Is she dying?
Might she want to break barriers?
Be my friend?
She had countertransference too.

I met someone, she says.
I mean really met someone.

She doesn't have cancer.

She continues.
The someone lives in Chicago.
Younger than I am.
A professor.
A little chunky, sexy though.

I am clearly not the intended recipient of this call.

I should say something.
I don't.
I want to hear more.
I don't want to hear more.

My ex-therapist is talking about herself
as if we're teenage girlfriends in the locker room.

This is wrong.
But I can't stop it.

For thirteen years I sleuthed her life,
figured out where she lived and with whom.

Now she's talking about the sex.

I am shrinking into my broken dining room chair,
feigning a smile she can't see.

I should be sitting on her leather couch
on East Seventh Street
talking about me,
about my deteriorating relationship,
my depleting self-esteem,

and how I've managed these eight years
with no therapist,

and how I really wish I had one I could call right now.

ALL BABIES CRY

Despite every flagrant glibness
Hysterical indignity: Juggling, kneeling,
Leaping, masticating.

Not one painstaking quest
Really solves the unconscionable
Vitriolic wailing.

Xanax yields zephyr.

MOM'S BIRTHDAY AT THE WOODSTOCK HOUSE

Fuck birthdays, says my mother.
Don't sit around staring at me, she tells my father, *go biking*.
I suggest brunch or a walk.
Fuck your father for not getting me anything but a fucking shirt and fuck him for going biking today.
Dad comes back after six hours.
You stink like an animal, she tells him.
I ask her what she'd like to do for dinner.
Price Chopper steak barbecue, suggests my father.
I'm not cooking a fucking thing, she says.
At the restaurant, she eats a burger and fries.
Nobody does a fucking thing for me, she says,
I'm a fucking doormat.

MR BEAGELMAN:

Why did you let me audition for all those plays?
Finian's Rainbow, Hair, Fiddler on the Roof,
Godspell. Until I was 13.
Never getting a part.
Belting out My Country 'Tis of Thee.
A cappella.
In my wispy voice. Alone
on stage. The empty auditorium.
And you, Mr. Beagleman with your clipboard, nodding.
In the third row.
Every year.
Every play.
Same song.

RAINY SUNDAY WITH TODDLER

Toilet paper strewn
the entire living room floor,

Twenty little metal cars,
In salad spinner. Spinning.

Half-eaten orange, crusted yogurt.
Sippy cup spillage.

The man with the yellow hat.
Curious George's friend or his captor?

Measuring spoons and garlic press under futon couch.
Dora tree house cookie episode,

For the fifteenth time. To-do list scraps,
shredded:

Postplacement pictures,
readoption, apples, tampons.

No more cookies, just fruit.
Baby Bop Barney bedtime book —

Guess What Time It Is — is an exclamation
not a question. Stupid book.

Dora is a cartoon.
The cat just shat.

I mean shoot.

BITCHES' BRITCHES

Shortly after the defunction of my father's
Kosher bicentennial fruitcake,
in nineteen seventy-six,
my parents decided it was time
to breed our standard poodle.
Theodora of Red Mill Farms was her name.
Theo for short.

This — after several years
of Theo's fertile blood drops
on the white tile hallway floor,
my mother, trailing behind her with a rag,
cursing my father.

And after my father discovered
that his underwear served an excellent additional purpose
to catch the blood, with a ready-made hole
for Theo's stubby tail. ("Who needs to buy *bitches' britches*
when you have Fruit of the Loom!" he boasted.)

It was a school night. I was eleven.
Theo was in heat.

The standard poodle stud
arrived with his humans
at our Henry Street apartment.
Like Theo, the stud had black curly hair,
which matched my mother's perm.

My father took his underwear off of Theo.
The grown-up humans stood in the living room
cajoling the dogs to meet.

I sat on the couch,
along the cleared living room perimeter,
my two-year-old sister next to me.

I watched, as the stud mounted my dog,
I watched, as the grown-up humans cheered.

PARENTS' BED AT THE WOODSTOCK HOUSE

It's a piece of shit, my mother says,
we have to replace it.
I sit, agreeing the bed is very hard and sharp.
My father calls out, *I can sleep on anything.*
You're a cheap fuck, she says.
I look underneath to see what gives.
The mattress is lodged
under the box spring.

MOMMY WRITING POEM NOW

I dream the child I adopt is really my big red cat.
He will never learn to read or speak English.

Rush to the Ethiopian doctor in Addis. Burning up.
No time for a shirt. No fever. Clearly your first, the doctor says.

Cousins Otto and Danitza adopt a baby girl from a Jewish
	agency
in the 1960s. *Poor girl got Danitza's nose anyway.*

Pregnant mothers of three discuss the pros and cons
Bugaboo chameleons, geckos, and frogs.

Blond movie star spotted at LA ball game
high fiving adopted black son.

Jane Abramowitz inherited Selma's nose job. Go figure.
Say hi Tinky Winky Dipsy Laa-Laa Po, Mommy writing
	now.

Otto's balls were shot off in World War II.
Danitza followed her daughter everywhere, hid behind trees.

When my son is five I'll be forty-five when he's thirteen
I'll be fifty-three when he's fifty-three I'll probably be dead.

Aurora, Arizona and Isis share bunny grahams at sing-along.
Mommy's putting tampon in now. Don't look.

White woman with black child seeks advice
from black woman with white child in Target elevator.

Danitza died after the cancer spread to her brain.
Her adopted daughter's eulogy was very moving.

Rumble and Tumble for Courageous Cubs is all booked up.
Mommy making cacka now.

Watch overweight pink plastic dinosaur sing unoriginal
    music.
Diddle diddle don't bite my tit when I change you.

In the dream, he rubs red fur against Baby Einstein
    discovery cards.
He vomits every day. He only loves me when he feels
    like it.

AGE RELATED

The pinguicula on my eyeball
is big today.
Angie had a TIA
Eric dropped dead.
I wonder if that's what grandma had
on *her* eyeball.

Lipomas just form — the doctor said —
usually not cancer.
I used to run ten miles, then six, then three,
now none.

Dawn's Nexium is starting to settle
in her small intestine,
making her anemic.

Iron is so constipating.

My girlfriend's ankle is swollen
and there's no sprain.

I must chew well,
so food doesn't get caught
in a diverticulum,

even if though hurts my teeth.

III

NORO VIRUS

I

It is airborne. Festering on doorknobs,
subway poles, toys, work files, toilet flushers.
I am on the D train. Too cold to bike,
damn winter.
I forgot my gloves and can't find a plastic bag.
I am trying to balance.
I breathe into my wool scarf.
This makes my glasses fog.
But moisture makes viruses spread.
I am confused about the best course.
A man is exhaling to my right,
I can feel his breath —
he has a greenish tint.
A child is licking the pole.

II

A text message yesterday informed me
that five-year-old Hazel

projectile vomited thirty minutes
after leaving a playdate at my house.
Which, according to her mother, she caught
from a cousin two days earlier.
There is contagion in my house.
Fuck shit fuck shit fuck shit.
My son may catch it.
I can catch it.
A two-day window of hibernation — this virus.
I bleached everything the child may have touched:
legos, sorry pawns, monster trucks.
I burned tea tree oil and sage throughout the house.
Ingested elderberry syrup, probiotics,
Xanax. Threw out the yo-yo,
enclosed Elmo in airless plastic.

III

My father called.
Are you well?
Did you speak to mom?
We both had it last night.
Did you get it? I could hear him laughing.
I told him *fuck you* and hung up.

YOUR FATHER HAS ALZHEIMER'S

Says my mother's message
on my answering machine.
Terrified, I can't bring myself to call her back.
I think about Dad wandering the streets
in his running shorts and down vest.
I swallow a Klonopin, make my girlfriend call.
She speaks to my mother, hands me the phone.
What are you nuts? says my mother,
Daddy forgot to go to Acme
to get the lox.

I HAD A WINDOW

I was a squatter
in hearing room 506.
The office was empty.
Claims for the space were under review, stalled
by state bureaucratic snarl.
I was bold, took what should be mine.
The other hearing officers were angry
that I — a transfer, of only a few months
could see the outside.
They filed petitions to the bosses in Albany.
Those without windows did not speak to me,
even to say hello.
The friends of those without windows
did not speak to me,
even to say hello.
My requests for an ergonomic chair
were thwarted.
But I had a window.
I could see scaffolding.
The tops of city buses. The swirling
litter of downtown Brooklyn.
I could see weather.

I was elated.
Then the email circulated.
I was being moved
to a small windowless nook
in the back northwest corridor of the fourteenth floor.
And now, this is where I sit.
Over the HVAC. Under
the yellow asbestos drenched tiles.
On my lopsided
ill-fitted
ergonomic chair.

BEDTIME POET

Last night, reading to my son
about *Hammer Heads*
and *Officer Buckle*,
I pretended that I was Louise Glück,
fading out slowly
at the ends of sentences
in a dreamy way.
And just like the night before,
last night, I fell asleep, mid-
sentence, in the warmth
of my little boy's bed.

CAREER CHANGE

The rabbi sleeps at the desk across the room.
Curly sidelocks drape along the ashtray.
The brown paneled office, above my father's
kosher bakery in Williamsburg, the week after
I was fired. I answer the phones. Macaroon King,
how may I direct your call?
The monitors are too old for screen saver.
The desk drawers have no handles.
The leather chairs are torn and hard.
Julio the barber next door lost his snake.
It's crawling somewhere in the bakery walls,
my father says maybe it will eat the rats.
The supermarket chain won't pay a nickel more
for a can. *Passover is killing us.*
Daytime Telemundo, on the bookkeeper's desk,
a woman weeps… *¡yo quiero matarme!*
The rabbi is snoring now,
but somehow, his yarmulke doesn't move.
Just across the river, lawyers in suits are eating
smoked turkey, swiss and avocado wraps,
with a honey mustard glaze. Checking their blackberries.
My father takes out two cans of sardines.

Skinless and boneless in olive oil.
We scoop them out with forks,
drink the oil.

ON MY FORTY-FIFTH BIRTHDAY

Leonardo is five. My son says.
And Layla and Sam and Jane and Arcadia,
they're all five too.
He starts to cry.
Why are you crying? I ask.
I want to be five.
Trust me, I tell him,
You will only be four once.
Enjoy four. Love four. I say.
Please (I am begging now.)
He cries harder.

I cry too.

SHRIMPS

My son is at the dining room table
spelling words.
I am helping him,
while I clean out the refrigerator.
I am multitasking.

I find spaghetti sauce from last week.
It can't be edible.
There are shrimps
in the sauce.
Shrimps go bad.

I heard on NPR that two-thirds
of the world's food is discarded.

I care about the environment.
I care about starving people.
And I don't compost.

I am the enemy.

But food, like feces, tampons
and fingernails,
is biodegradable.

I pour the sauce down the toilet.
The dead shrimps
will be reabsorbed by nature.
One less plastic bag.

I am good.

The toilet clogs.
Overflows.

My son asks what I am doing.
He needs three words that rhyme with it.

Spelling will have to wait.
I clean the floor.
Then I plunge.

And plunge.

SUBWAY SEAT

Sitting on this train,
I don't think about
what took place on this seat
an hour, a day, maybe even twenty minutes ago.
I don't think about the homeless person.
The bedbugs. The spit. The urine.
Except, that there's a faint funk.
And it seems to be coming from nowhere
but this seat.

A SUNDAY WALK IN AUTUMN

The leaves are dried up
in piles mixed with dog shit
and human trash.
The Ginkgo stinks
like sickness. Fuck
that extra hour of sleep.
Winter is coming,
and I am another
year older.

WATCHING ADOPTION VIDEO WITH MY EIGHT YEAR OLD

After a particularly shitty day in school
learning about immigration
then fighting with me
about reading logs, Minecraft and Hebrew school,
my son wants to watch his adoption video, again.

Given to us six and a half years earlier
by the Ethiopian social workers.

In the video, my son sees the hut he lived in,
his birth mother,
cows, a farm, an old grandmother.

The film culminates in meeting his adoptive mother — me.
He's not even two
but he's already my kid —
the Ethiopian courts had declared it.

All I'd seen before was a picture of his face.

Filmed by Elias, the cameraman at the care center
in Addis Ababa,

my son and I now watch as the adoptive mother
doesn't know how to pronounce her son's name.

She is smiling like a nervous idiot —
tries to hold the boy and he cries,
has no interest in the bubble wand in her hand.

You see — my son tells me
in our living room in Brooklyn
now sitting on my lap,
you are a stranger,
some random person.

IV

SPAM

The website of my poetry school
thinks I am spam.
Or at least, my IP address.
Not that I really understand
what that is.
But I am flagged.
Banned.
I do not sell Viagra.
I swear. I am a poet,
of sorts,
and I can't get on the poetry school website.
I would be an idiot,
if I did not see
the metaphor of this.

MACAROONS – THE LAST DAYS

The shop steward shows me her frozen toes.
Your father turned the heat off, again.

Cold is a state of mind, my father says.
In shorts and a muscle tank.

More complaints come in: a chemical taste.
Hard as a rock. Spoiled. Soapy.

Saponification: When coconut turns to soap.
A mystery, dad says.

My husband thinks I tried to poison him with your product,
a customer writes. *Please, tell him it's the coconut.*

Maybe you should, my father replies,
poison him.

Dad's knee is busted.
Doctors are fucking assholes, he says.

The other leg gives out.
He falls down the stairs.

The bookkeeper's skin is a greenish tint.
Lungs filled with fluid. Just got another stent.

Phone message from exterminator: Let your rats run wild,
Macaroon King, I don't work for free.

My father bolts the door,
so the rabbis can't get in.

We watch them buzz on the new
security TV. Purchased

after Jesus the mechanic
stole the computers.

PARENT/TEACHER CONFERENCE

My son's third grade music teacher
was the girlfriend of my piano teacher
in nineteen eighty-three.
I was a teenager.
She was hip and pretty with long hair.
She has no clue we ever met.
But I remember her.
I remember hearing her scat sing
while I walked up the stairs.
She also doesn't know
that I had sex with her thirtysomething boyfriend,
rather — that I let him have sex with me — after she'd leave
and after I played the Bach French Suites —
in their Bleeker Street walk-up.
I was desperately trying to be straight
(it didn't work.)
We are sitting on little kid chairs
and she is discussing my son's musical prowess,
in spite of his bad behavior in chorus.
She still has long hair, now dyed blond.
She tells me my son is a little lost,
struggling to find his place.

I know from lost — I want to yell out.
This conference is about my son.
So I nod and smile thinking
about being sprawled out numb
in nineteen eighty-three.
I want to talk about me.
I want to curl up into her arms
and go to sleep.

EXTRACTION

Tongue numb. Swelling
like anaphylaxis.
Blood stained bib

tight around my neck.
Long skinny needle prodding into —
puncturing my jaw. Suction

drying me out, slurping spit and snot.
I am practically upside down.
This dental dam may suffocate me.

It hurt for twenty-nine years.
In the '80s, it stank of decay.
(I sprayed it with Binaca.)

The ache, finally intolerable,
Dr. Mashman killed most of its nerve.
Though in a compromised state

(a crowned stub),
it lived through painting pipes
on kibbutz. Law school,

Midwest feminism, seventeen years of therapy,
chicken pox, rectal surgery.
Yesterday, it got scanned.

Dead, fractured, rotten,
infected to the bone.
Lower incisor left number twenty-eight

soon to be a big gaping hole.
Black thread stitching,
over sprinkled cadaver grafted bone.

SHIVA CALL

Fine, we're in the car, be outside at six, daddy
can't stand for you to take a cab,
starts mom's message,
are you farting again, you sick animal,
your father is disgusting,

make that 6:30,
daddy forgot his tooth.

NOBODY PUT A GUN TO MY HEAD

I wrote a poem last year that I wish I didn't write.
An embarrassing poem,
about allowing this older adult guy
to violate me, in a sense, when I was a teen.
Something I never talk about.
But when thirty years later that very same guy's girlfriend
from thirty years ago ends up as my kid's teacher,
I saw the art of the situation.
The irony was delicious
and repulsive.
So I wrote a poem.
I should have deleted the poem or at least filed it away.
I sent the poem out to magazines.
(What would be the chances?)
The poem was published.
And now, I can't take it back.
Nobody put a gun to my head.
I show the poem to no one,
hide the contributor copies.
I look on twitter.
The poem was tweeted.
I block the tweet.

An email from the editor
arrives in my inbox. A "superb" poem
was the feedback, he writes.
I delete the email.

FIFTY

Is when that box of tampons
purchased six months ago is still full.

When the AARP magazine makes for engaging
bathroom reading and an article like

How to Survive Your First Heart Attack
seems not so irrelevant.

Fifty is when you find yourself standing over an AC
even though outside it's negative three.

Fifty is when the parents who had you young
seem suddenly old — and you realize,

you're not far behind.
Fifty is when you can't remember

the last time you bought
a new bra. Not that you still bother to wear a bra.

Fifty Is The New Fat.

When you are closer to century
than fetus.

Fifty is when your kid calls you "grams"
just to fuck with you.

When the Benadryl in your cabinet expired
nineteen years ago.

Fifty is when your long-term relationship
which should have ended long ago,

must dissolve now because you both realize
there's so little time left.

Acknowledgments

The New Ohio Review: "Facebook Friends," "Parent/Teacher Conference" and "This is not an Obituary" (2018 Pushcart Prize Special Mention)

The Mom Egg Review: "Watching Adoption Video With My Eight Year Old"

Vine Leaves Literary Journal: "A Sunday Walk in Autumn"

Five to One #thesideshow: "Fuck Passover"

Rattle: "I Had a Window," "Taxi Court" and "Unemployment Judge"

Mudlark: "Career Change"

Fourteen Hills: "Subway Judge"

TriQuarterly: "Mommy Writing Poem Now" and "And Speaking of Strategic Planning"

New World Writing: "Fruitcake," "On the G Train" and "SPAM"

The Cape Rock: "Macaroons: The Last Days" (reprinted in The Writers Studio at 30, ed. Philip Schultz (Epiphany Editions 2017.)

Ping Pong: "Christmas at the Kosher Bakery" "Mom's Birthday at the Woodstock House" and "Your Father Has Alzheimer's"

Boston Literary: "Subway Seat" and "Extraction"

PANK: "Shrimps" (As for "Shrimps," I now compost. Compulsively)

Mohave River Review: "Music Festival," "Eric my Dead Friend" and "Nobody Put a Gun to My Head"

"On The G Train" was inspired by (and is a response to) Linda Gregg's poem "Bamboo And A Bird."

As for "Shrimps," I now compost. Compulsively

About the Author

Lisa Badner's writing has appeared in *Rattle, the New Ohio Review, TriQuarterly, Mudlark, The Satirist, PANK, Fourteen Hills, the Mom Egg Review, Ping Pong, New World Writing, Mohave River Review, Five to One*, and others. She received a Pushcart (2018) Special Mention. Lisa is a graduate of the University of Wisconsin and Brooklyn Law School and coordinates the tutorial program at the Writers Studio. She lives in Brooklyn with her teenage son and her chihuahua.

https://lisabadner.com